OVERCOMING ADDICTION™

ALCOHOL ABUSE

JENNIFER PETERS

Rosen
YA™

New York

D0204532

Published in 2019 by The Rosen Publishing Group, Inc.
29 East 21st Street, New York, NY 10010

First Edition

Library of Congress Cataloging-in-Publication Data

Names: Peters, Jennifer, 1985– author.
Title: Alcohol abuse / Jennifer Peters.
Description: New York : Rosen Publishing, 2019. | Series: Overcoming addiction | Includes bibliographical references and index. | Audience: Grades 7–12.
Identifiers: LCCN 2017045727| ISBN 9781508179382 (library bound) | ISBN 9781508179559 (pbk.)
Subjects: LCSH: Teenagers—Alcohol use—Juvenile literature. | Alcoholism—Juvenile literature. | Alcoholics—Rehabilitation—Juvenile literature.
Classification: LCC HV5135 .P48 2019 | DDC 616.86/106—dc23
LC record available at https://lccn.loc.gov/2017045727

Manufactured in the United States of America

CONTENTS

INTRODUCTION

When people think of alcohol abuse, they often think of older adults who knowingly drink too much. But the truth is many young people abuse alcohol as well, though often their friends and peers don't know because they don't fit the stereotype. The legal drinking age in the United States is twenty-one, while in Canada each province sets its own legal age; the drinking age is eighteen in Alberta, Manitoba, and Quebec, and nineteen in the other provinces. Today, though, most teens are familiar with alcohol even before these legal limits. According to the Centers for Disease Control and Prevention (CDC), nearly 33 percent of teens have tried at least one alcoholic beverage by the age of fifteen. By age eighteen, that number nearly doubles, to 60 percent. And those who start drinking at a younger age are six times more likely to develop alcohol-dependency issues later in life.

What does that mean for you?

Laws that cover underage drinking vary by state and by offense. While the legal drinking age makes it illegal for anyone under age twenty-one to possess alcohol, most states also make it illegal to purchase alcohol while underage, to drink alcohol, and to drive under the influence of alcohol. Getting caught doing

In the United States, the legal drinking age is twenty-one, but many teenagers first experiment with alcohol long before they reach legal age.

any of these things can result in a multitude of consequences. Legal consequences might include having to pay a fine or doing mandatory community service, having your driver's license suspended or revoked, or being sentenced to alcohol education or recovery.

Drinking, even for legal adults, is something that should happen only after you've thought through all the consequences. Being of age does not automatically make drinking alcohol OK. There are many things adults need to consider before taking a drink, including their dependency issues, how much they plan to drink, and whether they can drink without putting anyone else in danger, such as by drinking and driving.

While drinking isn't always a bad thing and does not always result in a negative outcome, it is something that should be thought through in advance, so that you can make the right decision for yourself. What you choose to do may not be the same as what your friends want to do. And that's OK.

Over the next few years, as you finish high school and go to college, the question of whether to drink or not will likely come up a lot, and you'll want to know what the best option is for you. Understanding the consequences of alcohol abuse will arm you with all the necessary facts so that you can make that decision when the time comes.

CHAPTER 1

TO DRINK OR NOT TO DRINK

Once you become a teenager, it can feel like alcohol is everywhere. You may notice the liquor cabinet in your house for the first time, or you may be offered a drink at a party. Your friends may be drinking beer on the weekends or sneaking a flask of alcohol into the prom. You might not even notice that it's happening at first. But when you do, you'll probably start to think about whether you want to take your first drink. And there are a lot of things that may make you choose one way over another.

Teens, like adults, have many reasons for choosing to drink alcohol. Some do it because their friends are doing it, and they don't want to feel left out. Others drink in the hopes that alcohol will help them forget that things aren't going well in their lives or will help them cope with those things. Some drink to try to loosen up, or be more carefree since alcohol can lower a person's inhibitions. And still others drink because they're bored and want to do something to end that boredom. Many people also drink just because they like the taste of certain alcoholic beverages.

Like adults, teenagers have many reasons for choosing to start drinking. Peer pressure is one of the most common reasons teenagers give for experimenting with alcohol while underage.

There is no "right" reason to drink alcohol, though most people would say that being of legal age and choosing to drink because you like the taste of a particular beverage is the only good reason. However, since that is rarely the kind of drinking that people view as problematic, it's important to consider the other reasons people turn to alcohol.

ALCOHOL IS NOT DUCT TAPE— IT CAN'T FIX EVERYTHING

Some people drink because they feel that they have too many other problems, and they are hoping that consuming alcohol will help them deal with those issues. This reason for drinking alcohol is especially true for teenagers, who are often dealing with more problems than their friends and parents realize, from the everyday problems of adolescence to more personal problems.

As a teenager, there are a lot of things going on in your life, including at home with your family, at school, and in your social life with your friends. Maybe your parents are going through a divorce, or the guy or girl you like at school isn't returning your attention. You might have had a fight with your best friend, or you could feel self-conscious about the way you look or how you dress. All of these are common problems, but they don't feel so common when you're going through them yourself. You can feel very alone. And some people use alcohol to try to erase those negative feelings and cheer themselves up.

Fights with your parents or dating troubles can seem terrible, but while alcohol may make you feel better in the moment, it can't fix the problems you're facing.

Alcohol can't fix your problems, but it can feel like it does when you're in the moment. Because alcohol lowers your inhibitions, drinking can make you feel more relaxed and comfortable. The reason alcohol makes you feel this way is because it stops two parts of your brain—the amygdala and the prefrontal cortex—from communicating efficiently with each other. The amygdala and prefrontal cortex are responsible for how people deal with emotion, so when those parts of your brain aren't talking to each other, it can be easier to feel less of the negative emotions that arise when you're sober.

If people drink every time they feel bad, and they feel fewer of those bad feelings while drinking, it's likely that they will associate the lack of negative feelings with the alcohol and will start thinking of alcohol as a positive influence on their emotional well-being. When this situation happens, they can develop a dependency on alcohol, in which they don't believe they can feel good without alcohol.

But alcohol can also have negative physical effects on the body. Drinking too much can increase your chances of developing liver disease. When your liver tries to break down alcohol, the chemical reaction it causes can inflame or damage liver cells. Alcohol can also damage your intestine, letting toxic gut bacteria get into your liver and cause damage.

Alcohol can cause less life-threatening but equally horrifying bodily effects, too. For instance, drinking causes dehydration, which is bad for your skin, and can lead to things like pimples or rosacea. Drinking in excess can also cause you to gain weight, as alcohol is converted to sugar in the body, and sugar is stored as fat.

ALCOHOL'S HIDDEN CALORIES

Even if you're not concerned with the negative health effects of drinking, you're probably going to want to think twice once you consider its effects on your appearance. Drinking can cause you to gain weight without you even realizing it. That's because people don't

(continued on the next page)

Alcohol has hidden calories and can cause you to gain weight, as the sugars in the drinks are converted directly to fat.

(continued from the previous page)

often consider all the calories hidden in their favorite drinks. But that beer or cocktail you had at a party contains just as many calories per gram as pure fat. A typical bottle of beer has an average of 142 calories. That's equivalent to eating half of a hamburger, and burning off those calories would take fourteen minutes of running. Meanwhile, two pints of beer would be 364 calories, or the equivalent of eating 1.2 hamburgers. So if you eat some chips and pizza at a party in addition to your drink, you could easily consume a full day's calories in one evening. Doing that often will cause you to gain weight, which, on top of the many health problems that can arise from drinking, can cause a number of other health problems.

EVERYONE DOES IT—OR SO IT SEEMS

Drinking can also be inspired by seeing other people drinking. It's very easy to feel like you're the only person who doesn't drink when you're at a party and other people are having a beer as if it's no big deal. No one wants to feel like the odd person out, especially during the teen and young adult years.

Some people drink because of peer pressure, or feeling driven to do what their friends do. You want your friends to like you, and if your friends tell you that drinking is cool or normal, you'll likely listen to them, even if you don't necessarily agree. Sometimes peer pressure comes from within, and you feel pressured to drink not because someone is telling you to, but because all of your friends are drinking in front of you. Even if they aren't saying you need to drink to fit in, you can feel that pressure just from watching them. And that's the case for both young people and adults. Fitting in is important, and feeling like an outcast can be incredibly uncomfortable. Even if you think you would never drink in most instances, if you see all your friends drinking, it's very easy to want to drink as well.

It's also easy to see drinking as something you can or should do if you see adults around you drinking. If your parents drink wine with dinner or go for a beer with their friends, it can feel like drinking is something adults do all the time. It may also make you feel like drinking is something that makes you an adult. And if adults are drinking, it doesn't seem like it's a bad thing because adults, you are often told, know what is best.

But just because everyone around you seems to be drinking, it doesn't mean they all are. You probably have friends who don't drink, though they may not talk about it very much, or at all. And your parents may drink only on special occasions, like holidays or at their annual Super Bowl party. It can seem like everyone around you is drinking, but if you stop and look around for a moment, you'll see that there are still plenty of people who don't have a drink in their hands.

THE COOL FACTOR

Related to peer pressure is advertising and celebrity pressure. Even if your friends aren't drinking at parties on Friday nights, and your parents don't have a full wine rack, you may still feel like you should be drinking because it's what you see happening in movies and on TV and what you hear about in popular music. You may see commercials for alcohol while streaming shows on Hulu or see characters on your favorite Netflix shows relaxing

Singer Lorde is one of many pop stars who have referenced alcohol in their song lyrics. This can make it seem as if drinking is cool or that everyone is doing it, when that's not necessarily true.

by having a few drinks at a bar. Lorde, Chance the Rapper, and other musicians mention alcohol in their songs, and there are memes of people tossing back a drink in response to bad news all over the internet. So even if everyone you know in your real life is sober, alcohol can seem like it's everywhere.

If you're uncertain about what you should be doing or how you should be acting to be cool and fit in, you're likely to look at what the people you think are cool are doing. So if the characters on *Riverdale* or *The Defenders* have a drink now and then, you may feel like you can or should be drinking, too. And if you are constantly hearing songs about having a drink in the club, it's going to seem like that's the thing to do.

Drinking is a huge part of popular culture. In 2017, *Time Out* magazine put out a list of the fifty best songs about drinking, and it barely scratched the surface. Almost every character on every television show about or for teenagers has had a drink at least once. Even characters on family-friendly shows like *The Fosters* have the occasional alcoholic beverage. When you're constantly seeing and hearing references to alcohol, it's easy to feel like everyone is drinking at least a little bit.

No matter why someone drinks, though, there is a difference between casual drinking and problem drinking. It's important to be aware of what constitutes problem drinking so you can seek help for yourself or for a friend who might be showing signs of alcohol dependency.

CHAPTER 2

TOO MUCH OF A "GOOD" THING

Regardless of why you choose to drink, whether it's to fit in, fix a problem, or just for fun, there is such a thing as problematic drinking—even if you're not underage. And drinking problems are not one size fits all. Different levels of drinking can be problematic for different people. For example, a recovering alcoholic could relapse from having just one drink, while someone who has three drinks at a party could be absolutely fine.

THE UNHAPPY CONSEQUENCES OF HAPPY HOUR

You need to know what happens when you drink too much. There are a number of physical, mental, and emotional issues that can arise from too much alcohol, and they can have varying effects on your daily life.

In terms of physical consequences, alcohol abuse can lead to a breakdown of your vital organs, an excess of fat on your liver,

Though you may feel happy and excited while drinking with friends, alcohol is a depressant, and once you've fully metabolized your drinks, you may find yourself more anxious or depressed.

cancer, heart disease, and stroke. You can also gain weight from drinking too much since the alcohol is metabolized as sugar in your body, and sugar is stored as fat. You may notice that you're developing more acne if you've been drinking too much, too.

Emotionally, you may find yourself feeling more anxious or depressed. Although in the midst of drinking, you might feel happy and excited, alcohol is a depressant and can lower your mood once it's fully entered your system. You might also notice that you have a cloudier mind and have a hard time focusing on things or concentrating on your work.

17

The depressive effects of alcohol can cause you to feel disconnected from friends and family, leaving you feeling isolated and alone.

If you're drinking too much, you might also feel that you have difficulties connecting to people. Because of the physical and emotional effects, you may feel generally bad when you're not drinking. That feeling could cause you to give up on things that used to matter to you, such as schoolwork, spending time with friends, or being with your family. You might lose interest in hobbies you enjoyed previously, or you may lose interest in everything, wishing only to drink and sleep.

If you or someone you know is experiencing any of these problems, you or that person might have an alcohol abuse problem. But now you're probably wondering, what constitutes alcohol abuse, and how will you know if you're drinking too much?

BINGEING: ONLY OK FOR TELEVISION

One of the biggest forms of problematic drinking, especially for teens, is binge drinking. Binge drinking is when a woman or girl drinks more than four drinks in one sitting and a man or boy drinks more than five. But why is bingeing bad?

Binge drinking may not seem like a problem every time someone does it. If you're out all night at a party, having four or five drinks may not seem like much at all. If you get to your friend's house at eight o'clock and have five drinks before you go home at midnight or later, you may feel fine. But how you feel and what has happened inside your body don't always match.

Binge drinking often results in the drinker feeling drunk. Being drunk means feeling any effects at all because of drinking. You might feel slightly dizzy when you're drunk, or you could feel nauseated and want to throw up. You could feel sick if you binge drink, or you might feel sleepy. Whatever it feels like, it means you are impaired. Being drunk means your body is not operating at its best, and you may make decisions different from those you would make if you were sober.

While everyone knows you're not supposed to drink and drive because driving while drunk can cause you to be a poor driver and get into an accident, there are a lot of other things

There are many negative effects of drinking, from feeling hungover and nauseous, to saying things you don't mean to say, to driving drunk and hurting yourself or someone else.

you can't or shouldn't do after you've been drinking. You could have a hard time walking in a straight line while drunk and could fall down the stairs. Or you could overcook your Hot Pockets if you use the microwave while drunk because you might not see the numbers on the touchpad as clearly. Or, as you've probably seen online and in TV shows and movies, you may say something you don't mean or want to say while drunk.

Although bingeing is characterized as problematic drinking, it is not always a sign of a real problem. If your dad has five beers over the course of the Super Bowl, but he doesn't drink much the rest of the year, it's not a problem, although he should be careful that day to avoid doing anything that will cause further harm. But if your friend drinks five or six drinks every time there's a party, it could be a sign that there's something more going on.

WHEN IS IT CONSIDERED TOO MUCH?

If you look only at binge drinking, you will assume that most people who drink in this way have a problem. Young people consume 90 percent of the alcohol they drink through binge drinking, according to the CDC. However, most people who binge drink are not alcohol dependent. So, if drinking too much is a problem, but not always, how do you know what "too much" really means?

One sign of a problem is the feeling that you have to have another drink. That feeling is different from the need to drink you may feel because of peer pressure. Rather, this feeling is that you need to drink for something to feel right. If you go to a party every Friday night and feel that you have to drink to have fun, that's a sign of problematic drinking habits. If any time there's alcohol around, you feel you have to drink it, regardless of the situation or whether or not you want to drink, it's a problem. If at any point you feel you need to drink and then do drink, you could be displaying signs of alcohol dependency.

Drinking to solve a problem is also a sign of dependency or abuse. If you drink every time you feel bad, it's a problem. You may have only one drink each time, but because you are drinking to fix something and to change how you feel, you are still displaying a kind of alcohol dependency. That's because you're relying on the alcohol to do something for you that it can't do: fix how you feel. So even if you have only one drink each time something goes wrong, you're still turning to alcohol instead of dealing with the underlying problem, which is a clear symptom of problem drinking.

WHO CAN BE AN ALCOHOLIC?

Many people assume alcoholics fit a particular stereotype. You might think of an alcoholic as someone who is dirty, unemployed, or a loner. Or you imagine that someone who abuses alcohol is someone who has nothing else going on in his or her life and who can't do anything right. But all kinds of people have drinking problems.

One of the biggest young stars of the twenty-first century, Daniel Radcliffe, admitted in 2012 that he had been drinking to the point of getting drunk since he was a young boy. Radcliffe is famous for playing Harry Potter in the blockbuster

Daniel Radcliffe became famous playing Harry Potter, but as a teenage star, the actor had a serious drinking problem and drank alcohol to help him "feel normal."

film franchise, but he confessed that as a young adult he was frequently drunk or hungover while filming.

It's probably difficult for people to imagine the sweet boy who played Harry Potter, the charming boy wizard, as having any problems at all. He became famous at age eleven and starred in one of the biggest film series in history, so what could possibly cause him to be an alcoholic? But Radcliffe told an interviewer that he drank in part to feel normal, especially after his work on the Harry Potter franchise ended and he had to figure out what came next in his life.

Pop singer Demi Lovato suffered from alcohol addiction as well. Although she's been in the limelight since childhood, starring first on *Barney and Friends* as a child and then becoming a Disney star famous for her role in the Camp Rock series of TV movies, Lovato's problem with alcohol was well hidden until she admitted to it in 2013.

Now an outspoken activist who helps other young women overcome eating disorders and substance abuse, Lovato was only a teenager when she started abusing alcohol and drugs. She's publicly admitted that she was nineteen when she realized her drinking had become problematic, but she still continued to drink. Lovato also admitted that she lied about her drinking so that those around her, including her mother, wouldn't know what was going on.

During those years, to an outside observer, Lovato was the perfect example of a sweet pop idol. She was in a serious relationship, starred in family-friendly films and television shows that were geared to tweens and teens, and was putting out songs that promoted confidence, happiness, and fun. Her confession in 2013 that she'd been suffering from alcoholism and drug addiction is proof that anyone can be a problem drinker.

Singer Demi Lovato became famous as a star of family-friendly Disney Channel shows and movies, but she admitted in 2013 that she abused alcohol and drugs as a teenager.

HOW WILL I KNOW?

If it sounds like there are a lot of ways for someone to hide drinking habits, you're right. As discussed earlier, different situations can be problematic for different reasons. If you don't know how someone drinks every time that person drinks, you can think a person who has one drink each time you see him or her has no problem at all, while a person you see binge drinking once every six months seems like a person in need of help. So how do you know the difference?

One of the biggest things to look for is the effect alcohol is having on your life or the life of the person you're concerned about.

Someone who has a problem with alcohol abuse or dependency will see the effects in his or her everyday life, even when he or she is not drinking. For example, a report by Harvard University found that college students who binge drink are as much as eight times more likely to miss classes and fall behind in their schoolwork than their peers are. So if you notice that your friend who drinks a little too much is starting to skip class or show up late, or if his or her work seems to be of lower quality, it could be a result of problematic drinking.

Another sign that someone is drinking too much could be in how he or she explains his or her drinking. If that person celebrates every good thing with a drink or needs to have a drink every time something goes wrong, he or she may be developing alcohol dependency. Even if that person only has one or two drinks each time, the fact that drinking is the first thing he or she **thinks to do is a sign that his or her relationship to alcohol is not a healthy one.**

Constant hangovers or illnesses can also point to an alcohol abuse problem. Drinking to excess can weaken your immune system, making you more susceptible to all kinds of illnesses, from the common cold to more serious ailments, such as tuberculosis and pneumonia. Of course, you don't have to get too sick to know there's a problem. If you consistently feel tired, have dry mouth and eyes, or develop a headache after drinking, and you continue to drink regularly, you're exhibiting signs of having a problem.

While many of these signs could be visible in someone who is a casual drinker, an important thing to look at is whether the problems drinking causes stop the person from drinking more. If you notice that your grades are slipping because you're drinking too much and having trouble staying awake in class the next day, but you continue to drink, you have a serious problem. If, however, you find yourself feeling sick every time you drink and so you stop drinking, you're on the right track.

MYTHS AND FACTS

MYTH: Alcoholics just need to try harder to stop drinking.

FACT: While recovering from alcohol abuse involves a great deal of willpower, alcoholism is an illness that has many factors, including genetic predisposition and psychological wellness. It is a disease, and treatment can involve a number of steps.

MYTH: You'll know someone is an alcoholic because he or she is a mess in all areas of his or her life.

FACT: It's often impossible to tell whether someone has alcohol abuse issues just by looking at him or her. Many problem drinkers can still go about their everyday lives without giving away any clues to their issues and often will work hard to hide their problems to prevent anyone from realizing there's something wrong.

MYTH: You have a problem drinking only if you hit rock bottom.

FACT: Many people realize they themselves or their loved ones have a problem with alcohol long before they hit rock bottom. There are people who stop drinking before it becomes a problem because they feel that continuing to drink will be too harmful. You don't need to be an alcoholic to realize you have an alcohol abuse issue and to change your habits.

CHAPTER 3

HOW TO LEND A HELPING HAND

It's not always easy for people to admit they have problems. If you know someone who seems to have an alcohol addiction, and you want to help, there are many steps you can take to help him or her.

The most important thing many recovery experts point out is that alcoholism isn't rational. While you may see your friend as having a problem and be able to point to why his or her drinking is hurting him or her and how, your friend probably doesn't see it the same way. There are many things that make someone start to drink, and those are not rational reasons. Whatever is causing the loved one in your life to drink too much, he or she usually cannot be reasoned into stopping. You will not be able to fix his or her dependency issue by telling your loved one that his or her drinking is a problem, although it can help jump-start a path to recovery.

So, what can you do to help?

If you're worried that a friend has been abusing alcohol, the first step is to talk to her. Tell her you're concerned, and ask if there's anything you can do to get her help.

TALK IT OUT

The first thing to do is to talk with your friend about your concerns. You may think your friend realizes his or her drinking is a problem and is affecting his or her life, but in the midst of alcoholism, he or she may not actually see what you do. But you can't confront your friend in an angry or combative way.

If you're going to speak to someone about a perceived alcohol addiction, you should find a private place to discuss your concerns with him or her. You don't want to embarrass your friend or put him or her on the defensive, so finding a time when you can speak in private and without interruption will give you a better chance to communicate openly. If there are other people in your friend's life who are concerned, you can also get them involved in the conversation.

Many would call this group chat an intervention, but there are people who would feel attacked in a traditional intervention setting. Instead, you want to make the conversation as relaxed and friendly as possible. While you are going to be telling your loved one that you believe he or she has a problem, you don't want your loved one to feel that you are picking a fight.

Instead, you want to tell your friend that you love and care for him or her and that you're worried about him or her. You can list some of the signs you've seen, and tell your friend that you believe those signs point to a bigger problem. But do not be surprised if your friend tells you you're wrong. It is very difficult to admit to a personal shortcoming, and your friend may think you're saying that he or she is doing something wrong or is failing in some way. This is not the case, so do your best not to refer to his or her drinking problem as a fault or something for which he or she needs to take the blame for.

OFFER HELP, BUT DON'T FORCE IT

You cannot make someone do something he or she isn't ready for. So if you sit down and talk to your friend and he or she doesn't believe you or refuses to admit he or she has a problem, you can't force him or her to do so. To recover from addiction, the addict needs to be willing to admit he or she has a problem. But if your friend refuses to admit he or she may be drinking too much, that does not mean you have to give up.

HOW TO STAGE AN INTERVENTION

If you're worried about a friend's drinking, you may consider holding an intervention to confront your friend about his or her drinking problem. If this is something you want to do, the Mayo Clinic offers a few steps to help you.

Confronting a friend about his or her drinking problem might be scary, but staging an intervention is one of the best ways experts have come up with to help addicts realize their problem and start on the path to getting help.

The first step is to make a plan. You'll want to talk to other people who may be concerned, such as other friends, family members, or your friend's boyfriend or girlfriend. You may also want to reach out to a counselor to help guide you and the group through the intervention.

Next, you need to gather information. You'll want to discuss with the group you've gathered beforehand how bad your friend's drinking has become and what sort of effects this is having on his or her life. You'll also want to read up on alcohol abuse and treatment so that you can present your friend with solutions and not simply the problem.

You should also come up with consequences for your friend, which you and other group members can enforce. And after the intervention, you'll want to follow up with your friend and keep your word about consequences or he or she won't take your concern seriously.

Recovery specialists discuss enabling a great deal. One of the immediate steps you and other friends can take if you have a loved one with a drinking problem is to stop helping him or her hide that problem. Even if your loved one refuses to get help, you can help him or her by stopping any behavior that allows him or her to keep drinking. Maybe you see your friend is drinking too much when you go to parties on Friday nights. If that's the case, you can stop inviting your friend out with you. Or maybe you find that your friend has to borrow money whenever he or she wants a drink because your friend has spent all of his or hers. If you're constantly lending him or her money, stop. Perhaps your friend asks you to cover for him or her when late for class because of a hangover or suggests you lie to his or her parents to keep your friend's partying habits secret. But if you want to help your friend, you have to stop helping that friend in the ways he or she wants.

It will not be easy to cut your friend off, especially if you are particularly close. You may miss getting to spend time with that friend, or your friend may get mad at you for not doing what he or she wants. Your friend could take your refusal to help him or her get drunk as a refusal to be his or her friend. Your friend may hurt your feelings if he or she chooses to fight you on this. But if you want to truly help a person with an alcohol dependency issue, you have to stop enabling that person. If you continue to do the things that you did with him or her when your friend started drinking, he or she will continue to drink because it's easy. Addiction is a battle against what is easy and what comes naturally.

TAKING THE NEXT STEP—OR TWELVE

Once you stop enabling your friend's behavior, he or she will either start to see the problem, or he or she will continue to fight. If your friend chooses to take another look at his or her actions and see that he or she has a problem with alcohol abuse, a good next step is to volunteer to go with your friend to a meeting for people struggling with alcoholism. You can take your friend to an Alcoholics Anonymous (AA) meeting, a well-known organization of groups of people of all ages and lifestyles who have abused alcohol who come together to help and support each other, or to a similar group meeting.

Many local community centers, like churches, town halls, and schools, host AA meetings, for alcoholics, and Al-Anon meetings, for the family and friends of problem drinkers. There are even special teen meetings, Alateen, for teens who have been affected by someone else's drinking.

If your friend doesn't want to attend a meeting by himself or herself, you can attend an Alateen meeting. Designed for teens and young adults whose loved ones have problems with alcohol, Alateen meetings can introduce you to other people who have been in your shoes. You'll be able to learn more about alcoholism and ways to help your friend, as well as how to help yourself and how to deal with your friend's drinking.

CHAPTER 4

LEARNING TO HELP YOURSELF

If you're the one with the drinking problem and you want to seek help, there are myriad resources available to you. While AA is the most popular option for overcoming an alcohol addiction, there are many other programs that can help you curb or quit your drinking.

ONE STEP AT A TIME

The most readily available option for teens who want to quit drinking is AA. Because most community centers host meetings, you can probably find several meeting groups in your neighborhood by looking online. Meetings are anonymous, which means no one has to know anything about you other than your first name and your drinking habits, and they are free and open to everyone. There are meetings every day of the week and at all different times, and most are hosted in churches and schools, so you will likely be able to find a meeting nearby.

Alcoholics Anonymous created the now famous twelve-step program that the majority of treatment centers and programs use when helping drug and alcohol abusers overcome their addictions.

AA works by taking participants through a twelve-step program with help from a sponsor, or mentor, as well as regular attendance at group meetings, where people receive support from others who have been through the program.

The twelve steps in AA's program are designed to help the participants admit their problem and then work to overcome their drinking and repair the damage done in their lives by their drinking.

Step one involves alcoholics admitting that they are powerless over alcohol's influence on their lives and that they need help. Steps two and three ask the participant to ask God for help and give God power over their lives. However, a belief in God is not required; AA members can substitute anything they want for God, as long as they are willing to admit they have a problem and ask for help. Steps four and five involve the alcoholic taking a long, hard look at his or her life and looking at the ways alcohol has affected him or her and those around him or her.

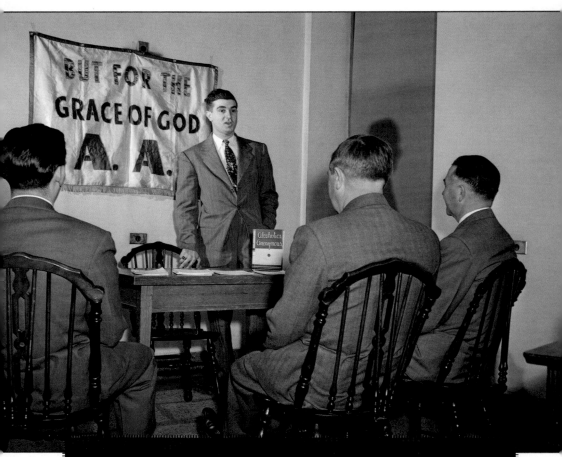

Members of AA attend meetings, where they get support and help from fellow addicts and those who have overcome their addictions.

Steps six and seven once again require the alcoholic to look to a higher power for help, though that power can be anything and does not need to be God or any deity. In step eight, the alcohol abuser must make a list of all the people who have been hurt by his or her drinking, and in step nine, the alcoholic must make amends to those people and ask for forgiveness. Steps ten, eleven, and twelve all involve continuing the journey to sobriety by reevaluating habits and behaviors and reflecting on the things that the alcoholic can do to help himself or herself and others.

Although AA doesn't always work, and it isn't going to work for everyone, it is so far the most effective treatment plan that has been developed for addicts. In the more than eighty years since AA was started by Bill Wilson (known as Bill W. within the anonymous program), thousands of people, if not millions, have used the program to overcome their addictions to not only alcohol, but also drugs, food, and sex. The program's twelve steps have been adapted to work for many kinds of addictions and many kinds of addicts, so that there is a form of AA out there for anyone who believes he or she needs it. And with more than sixty-one thousand meetings taking place around the United States and five thousand in Canada, most people can find a group for themselves.

AROUND-THE-CLOCK RECOVERY

For some people, however, just being in AA isn't enough. The program is based on free and open meetings, but an addict may feel that he or she needs a little more intensive help than is provided in AA meetings. For those people, there are inpatient recovery programs that can help addicts overcome their addictions.

An inpatient recovery center requires the addict to commit to constant recovery and often involves living at the center for anywhere from several weeks to several months. These types of programs can be expensive, but they also give you around-the-clock access to addiction counselors and cut you off from the lifestyle, people, and places that affected or influenced your drinking. By immersing yourself in sobriety all at once, some people believe you have a better shot at overcoming the addiction, whereas if one is only participating in an AA-type program, some feel that there is too much room to continue problematic behaviors.

For some people, meetings and therapy aren't enough to overcome addiction. For people who need more, clinics like the Betty Ford Center can provide care twenty-four hours a day, seven days a week.

Some of the best-known addiction recovery facilities are the Betty Ford Clinic and the New York-based Daytop Village. While Betty Ford is open to everyone, Daytop is especially known for its work with young adults and their families.

At these facilities, rehabilitation is personalized for each participant, and patients are given full, well-rounded treatment options, including treatment for physical and emotional issues that arose from their drinking. For young patients, classes are provided so students don't fall behind in school while going through recovery.

Like AA, inpatient treatment facilities rely on group meetings and twelve-step programs to help patients overcome their addictions. However, at these facilities medical doctors, psychologists, and recovery specialists also aid patients to help them work through the many facets of their addictions. These live-in centers work with addicts to help them not only to overcome their problematic behaviors, but also to regain the parts of their lives and health that were jeopardized by their addictions.

GOING PRO

If you don't think that a live-in recovery program would be best for you, but you want more help than Alcoholics Anonymous groups can provide, you can find a hybrid in an outpatient treatment program. Outpatient programs work like AA, with recovering addicts attending group meetings and sharing their progress with other recovering addicts. However, these groups are typically led by mental health or recovery professionals, adding an extra level of help that most AA meetings don't have.

If you're uncertain which type of program would most benefit you, you can start by attending a local AA meeting and talking to the group facilitator there. Often the people in AA meetings have been in recovery for a long time, and they may be able to tell you more about the group they lead and what other programs are in your area that could help you. You can also look up an accredited addiction counselor online and find someone in your city or state who has received training and has worked with other addicts before.

Whatever you choose for yourself, recovery will succeed only if you're willing to work at it.

TEN GREAT QUESTIONS
TO ASK AN ADDICTION COUNSELOR

1. What are some ways to reduce the effect of triggers that cause me to drink?

2. What are things I can do instead of drinking when I feel anxious or depressed or want to celebrate something?

3. How can I tell my friends that I don't want to drink without them thinking I'm judging them for drinking?

4. How do I tell my family and friends that I have a problem with drinking and want to get help?

5. If I suspect a friend or loved one has an alcohol abuse problem, what can I say to him or her to let that person know I care for him or her without making him or her feel that I'm judging him or her for the problem?

6. I'm scared to go to an AA meeting. What can I do on my own to get started on the path to recovery without seeking assistance from a group?

7. I'm worried about people judging me when they find out I have a drinking problem. What do I say to people to explain why I need to be sober?

8. Will my alcoholism ever be cured or will I have to work at this my whole life?

9. I only drink socially, when I'm out with my friends or at a party. How can I still have a problem if I'm not drinking all the time?

10. What are the effects of alcohol abuse on the rest of my life?

A CHANCE TO START OVER

Once you have committed to recovery, or your friend has, there are many things you can look forward to, like getting your life back and getting healthy again. But what sort of things change when you quit drinking?

Drinking puts you at risk for a number of health problems, including such terrifying things as cirrhosis of the liver, stroke, cancer, heart disease, and high blood pressure. When you quit drinking, your liver has a chance to detox, you'll see your skin become clearer, you may lose weight, and you'll even start to sleep better.

According to the National Institute on Alcohol Abuse and Alcoholism, drinking is also the cause of more than 4,000 deaths of people under age twenty-one each year, and quitting will help you avoid becoming a statistic. Of those young adults killed in connection with alcohol consumption, more than 1,500 die in car accidents, more than 1,200 in homicides, nearly 500 from suicide, and more than 200 from alcohol poisoning, falls, burns,

Overcoming addiction isn't easy, but once you've started to recover, you're likely to feel healthier and happier. You may start doing better in school or regaining interest in old hobbies.

or drowning. While quitting drinking doesn't mean you will never suffer the consequences, it does mean you are less likely to be a victim of an alcohol-related crime or illness.

Of course, the benefits won't happen overnight. In the beginning, you may even notice some negative side effects, known as withdrawal symptoms. Your symptoms will vary depending on the volume and frequency of your drinking, but you may experience more anxiety and depression, insomnia, tremors, or shaking of your hands or limbs, irritability, or hallucinations. If this happens, don't give up. Remember why you wanted to stop drinking and reach out to a friend, family member, or trusted doctor or counselor to help you until your symptoms subside and you feel like yourself again.

WHAT DO I DO NOW THAT I'M SOBER?

As you start to recover from your alcohol dependency, you'll notice that things in your life are changing. Not only will your health improve as the weeks and months pass, but your ability to participate in all areas of your life will improve. You'll have more energy to spend quality time with your friends and family, and you'll likely start doing better in school as the effects of alcohol wear off.

But being sober can be difficult when you've grown accustomed to drinking regularly, and you'll need to relearn how to socialize and handle problems without turning to alcohol. So how do you do that?

If your friends still drink, you won't be able to hang out with them in the same way you did before since being around alcohol and people drinking could cause you to relapse. Instead, you'll need to find new things to do when you want to spend time with your friends. Maybe that means going out to eat or going to see a movie. You could also take up healthy activities that your friends can join you in, such as a yoga, meditation, or exercise class.

You might also mistakenly believe that you can't have fun without drinking, especially if you've become used to drinking whenever you have fun. But chances are, your drinking had very little to do with the amount of fun you had with your friends. More likely, it was the people you enjoyed and the activities you participated in together, like dancing, singing karaoke, or joking around.

Almost all of the things you did while drinking can still be part of your life once you get sober.

YOU ARE NOT ALONE

While giving up your bad habits can be difficult and lonely at times, you will most likely have support from your friends and family in the process, and you'll make new friends as you regain your life in sobriety.

Celebrities like Demi Lovato and Daniel Radcliffe have overcome addiction, as mentioned earlier in this book, as have people like Oprah, rapper Eminem, singer Britney Spears, and actress Drew Barrymore. All of these stars not only managed to work through their addictions and regain their lives, they also went on to major success in their fields. But they had to work to figure out how to live without alcohol or drugs, just like anyone struggling with addiction.

"I had to learn the hard way that I can't do parties anymore," Lovato told the website Refinery29 in 2016. "Some people can go out and not be triggered, but that's not the case for me." Though one of the most popular young celebrities in Hollywood, at age twenty-three, Lovato had to stop doing the things that so many other young starlets take for granted to protect her sobriety.

Other celebrities choose sobriety even though they don't have an addiction problem. People like actress Blake Lively and singer Jennifer Hudson have chosen not to drink not because

Though she doesn't have an addiction issue, Jennifer Hudson chooses to be sober for her overall health.

of an addiction issue, but because they don't see the benefit of consuming alcohol. Even Kim Kardashian, who has done advertisements for alcohol companies in the past, doesn't drink.

WORKING TOWARD A LIFETIME OF SOBRIETY

Even if you have no problem kicking your alcohol addiction at first, or your friend doesn't, it will take a lifetime of work to remain sober. Maintaining your sobriety takes a daily commitment. You will need to learn about the things that trigger your behavior and make you want to drink again, and you'll need to find ways to avoid those triggers or counteract them. You'll also have to surround yourself with people who are willing to help you stay sober, be they family and friends, fellow recovering addicts, doctors, counselors, or a combination of all of those.

But as you've learned, there are many benefits to cutting back or quitting drinking. Your health will improve greatly when you give up your addiction—not just your physical health, your mental and emotional health will improve as well. You'll also see improvements in areas of your life that may have been neglected while you were under the influence of alcohol. As you become more comfortable living a sober lifestyle, you'll begin to feel more comfortable in class and with your friends, and you'll start to learn new things about yourself, such as discovering a love of yoga or a taste for foods you hadn't eaten before, because you'll be experiencing life in a new way.

As you work toward figuring out whether you have a problem with alcohol abuse, or a loved one does, you'll have to consider all the things you've learned so far, from the signs of addiction, to the effects of addiction, to the possible outcomes.

Kelly Osbourne, a television presenter, struggled with alcohol abuse as a young adult. It took her six years to overcome her addictions, proving that kicking a bad habit is not easy, but it can be done.

According to the National Epidemiologic Survey on Alcohol and Related Conditions (NESARC), the largest-ever survey on alcohol abuse, only 30 percent of alcoholics who try to quit are successful in giving up drinking for good. Many people need to try numerous times before they are able to give up their addictions. Kelly Osbourne, a former reality show star, singer-songwriter, actress, fashion designer, and television presenter, needed six years of trying before she was able to kick her addiction to drugs and alcohol. During that time, she went to rehab four times, went through six detoxes, and was checked into a mental health facility once before she finally committed to remaining sober.

If you don't succeed in giving up alcohol on the first try, or your friend can't, do not give up. It may take several tries, and lots of time living and working while sober or seeking sobriety, before you're able to beat your addiction. But lots of young people—both celebrities and everyday young men and women—have overcome alcohol abuse and gone on to live full and happy lives.

As you work through your sobriety and move toward living a life without alcohol, it's important to be aware of all the resources that are available to you and all the people in your support system whom you can turn to for help. Don't be afraid to talk to someone close to you and tell him or her how you feel, about either your drinking or someone else's.

While it can be difficult to take the first step, you are now armed with all the information and resources you need to figure out what the best thing is for you at this moment in time.

GLOSSARY

ADDICTION COUNSELOR A professional with experience working with alcoholics and other addicts and helping people through the recovery process.

AL-ANON A group connected to Alcoholics Anonymous that focuses on helping the friends and family members of alcoholics and recovering alcoholics.

ALCOHOL ABUSE An overreliance on alcohol; sometimes used interchangeably with alcoholism.

ALCOHOLIC A person with a dependence on alcohol.

ALCOHOLICS ANONYMOUS (AA) A nonprofit organization started in 1939 that exists to help people who suffer from alcohol addiction learn how to get sober and live a life free of alcohol.

ALCOHOLISM An illness that is caused by a dependence on alcohol. Many factors contribute to alcoholism, including genetics, surroundings, upbringing, and mental health.

AMYGDALA Like the prefrontal cortex, the amygdala can be damaged by excess drinking, which impedes critical thinking, memory, and emotional response.

BINGE DRINKING Drinking more than four drinks (for women) or five drinks (for men) in a short period of time. The time associated with bingeing varies depending on the source but can be anywhere from four to five drinks in two hours to four to five drinks in one evening.

CALORIES Units of energy that are derived from the food and drinks you consume; alcohol has no nutritional value and therefore is considered to contain "empty" calories.

CIRRHOSIS A liver condition that arises after long-term trauma to the organ; it is frequently caused by alcoholism and can lead to complete liver failure or death.

DEPENDENCY A condition in which a person cannot function normally without help from something; alcohol dependency refers to a reliance on alcohol.

INPATIENT Describing a treatment facility where patients get care twenty-fours a day and seven days a week.

INTERVENTION A group meeting arranged by the friends and loved ones of someone who has developed a drinking or drug problem to confront the person about his or her addiction.

LIVER The organ in your body responsible for breaking down alcohol and drugs before passing your blood on to the rest of your body.

OUTPATIENT Describing a treatment facility where patients go for regular care and meetings but continue to live on their own.

PEER PRESSURE When you feel that you have to do something because all of your friends are doing it or are telling you to do it, especially if you wouldn't do the thing without your friends' influence.

PREFRONTAL CORTEX The prefrontal cortex is a part of the brain that is responsible for planning, decision making, and moderating social behavior. Alcohol can prevent the prefrontal cortex from carrying out these activities.

REHABILITATION An experience of returning to the way you were before developing alcoholism; rehabilitation is generally accepted as including meetings, counseling, and assistance from medical and mental health professionals.

SOBER Not using drugs or alcohol. Sober can apply to a particular moment or to a lifestyle lived without drugs or alcohol.

FOR MORE INFORMATION

Alcoholics Anonymous (AA)

AA World Services, Inc.

475 Riverside Drive, 11th Floor

New York, NY 10115

(212) 870-3400

Website: https://www.aa.org

Facebook: @1StepAtTheTime

Twitter: @AlcoholicsAA

AA is a nonprofit organization, founded in 1939, that seeks to help alcoholics and recovering alcoholics in their search for sobriety. The organization started the famous Twelve-Step Program that is used in almost all other addiction treatment programs around the world.

Al-Anon

Al-Anon Family Group Headquarters, Inc.

1600 Corporate Landing Parkway

Virginia Beach, VA 23454-5617

(757) 563-1600

Website: https://al-anon.org

Email: wso@al-anon.org

Facebook: @AlAnonFamilyGroupsWSO

Twitter: @AlAnon_WSO

Connected to Alcoholics Anonymous, Al-Anon is a nonprofit organization that works to help the families and friends of alcoholics and recovering alcoholics. They assist these people in learning how to deal with their loved one's addiction and how to move past it.

Canada Drug Rehab
Sunshine Coast Health Centre
2174 Fleury Road
Powell River, BC V8A 0H8
Canada
(877) 746-1963
Website: http://www.canadadrugrehab.ca
Canada Drug Rehab is a public search tool and helpline, sponsored by the Sunshine Coast Health Center, that helps Canadian citizens search for treatment facilities and meetings in their province or city. The site includes searches for alcohol, drug, sex, gambling, and eating disorder recovery options and allows users to search for programs that will meet their individual recovery and economic needs.

Canadian Centre for Addictions
20 De Boers Drive, Suite 208
North York, ON M3J0H1
Canada
(855) 499-9446
Website: https://www.canadiancentreforaddictions.org
Email: info@ccfatreatment.org
Twitter: @CDRhelpdesk
A private addiction recovery facility, the Canadian Centre for Addictions is a top-rated treatment center located in Ontario that assists patients in overcoming alcohol and drug addiction, including addiction to prescription drugs.

Daytop New Jersey
360 Mount Kemble Avenue
Morristown, NJ 07960
(862) 260-9460

Website: http://daytopnj.org
Email: info@daytopnj.org
Facebook: @daytopnewjersey
Twitter: @daytopnj80
A rehabilitation and addiction recovery center located in New Jersey, Daytop primarily treats teenagers and young adults who suffer from addiction and works with their families to ensure a successful recovery.

Hazelden Betty Ford Foundation
PO Box 11
Center City, MN 55012-0011
(866) 261-3734
Website: http://www.hazeldenbettyford.org
Email: info@hazeldenbettyford.org
Facebook: @hazeldenbettyfordfoundation
Twitter: @hazldnbettyford
Named for former First Lady Betty Ford, wife of President Gerald Ford, the Betty Ford Center is a world-renowned recovery facility with locations across the United States. Betty Ford founded the center after she recovered from her own alcohol addiction in the 1970s.

FOR FURTHER READING

Ambrose, Marylou, and Veronica Deisler. *Investigating Alcohol*. New York, NY: Enslow Publishing, 2015.

Etingoff, Kim. *Drugs and Alcohol*. Broomall, PA: Mason Crest, 2015.

Henneberg, Susan. *Defeating Addiction and Alcoholism*. New York, NY: Rosen Publishing, 2016.

Landau, Jennifer. *Helping a Friend with an Alcohol Problem*. New York, NY: Rosen Publishing, 2017.

Meyer, Terry Teague. *I Have an Alcoholic Parent. Now What?* New York, NY: Rosen Publishing, 2015.

Newell, Ella. *The Hidden Story of Alcoholism*. New York, NY: Rosen Publishing, 2014.

Parker, Chance. *A Kid's Guide to Drugs & Alcohol*. Vestal, NY: Village Earth Press, 2016.

Parks, Peggy J. *The Dangers of Alcohol*. San Diego, CA: ReferencePoint Press, 2017.

Poole, Hilary W. *Drug and Alcohol Dependence*. Broomall, PA: Mason Crest, 2016.

Steinberg, Neil, and Sara Bader. *Out of the Wreck I Rise: A Literary Companion to Recovery*. Chicago, IL: University of

BIBLIOGRAPHY

Al-Anon Family Groups. "What Is Al-Anon and Alateen?" Retrieved December 18, 2017. https://al-anon.org /newcomers/what-is-al-anon-and-alateen.

Alcoholics Anonymous, "The Twelve Steps." Retrieved December 18, 2017. https://www.aa.org/assets/en_US/en_tt_contents .pdf.

Brittany. "Closing Your Tab—Natural Alternatives to Alcohol." Sober College, August 10, 2015. http://sobercollege.com /addiction-blog/alternatives-to-alcohol.

Centers for Disease Control and Prevention. "Fact Sheet—Binge Drinking." June 7, 2017. https://www.cdc.gov/alcohol /fact-sheets/binge-drinking.htm.

Centers for Disease Control and Prevention. "Fact Sheet— Underage Drinking." October 20, 2016. https://www.cdc.gov /alcohol/fact-sheets/underage-drinking.htm.

Choices Recovery. "5 Common Myths About Alcoholism." December 15, 2015. http://crehab.org/blog /addiction/5-common-myths-about-alcoholism.

Conan, Neal. "Alcoholics Anonymous: 75 Years of 12 Steps." NPR, July 22, 2010. http://www.npr.org/templates/story /story.php?storyId=128696654.

-facts/health-effects-of-alcohol/mental-health
/alcohol-dependence.

Drinkaware. "Unit & Calorie Calculator."Retrieved December 18, 2017.   https://www.drinkaware.co.uk/understand-your
-drinking/unit-calculator.

Drinkaware. "What to Expect When You Stop Drinking." Retrieved December 18, 2017. https://www.drinkaware.co.uk/advice
/how-to-reduce-your-drinking/how-to-cut-down
/what-to-expect-when-you-stop-drinking.

Gillette, Sam. "Kelly Osbourne Reveals She Was Once Committed to a Mental Institution—How Drug Abuse Got Her There." *People*,   April   25,   2017.   http://people.com/books
kelly-osbourne-once-committed-mental-institution
-drug-abuse.

Hazelden Betty Ford Foundation "Breaking Myths About Alcoholism." July 24, 2016. http://www.hazeldenbettyford
.org/articles/breaking-myths-about-alcoholism.

HealthTalk.org. "Young People's Experiences." January 2015. http://www.healthtalk.org/young-peoples-experiences
/drugs-and-alcohol/advice-young-people-about-drugs-and
-alcohol.

Huffington Post. Celebrity. "28 Celebrities Who Have Admitted They Don't Drink." January 23, 2014. http://www.huffington
post.com/2013/12/18/sober-celebrities_n_4467722
.html?slideshow=true.

Mayo Clinic. "Intervention: Help a Loved One Overcome Addiction." July 20, 2017. http://www.mayoclinic.org
/diseases-conditions/mental-illness/in-depth/intervention
/art-20047451.

Morris, Meagan. "Study Shows Why Alcohol Lowers Our Inhibitions." SheKnows, September 6, 2013. http://www

.sheknows.com/health-and-wellness/articles/1016655 /study-shows-why-alcohol-lowers-our-inhibitions.

National Institutes of Health. "Alcohol and the Immune System." Retrieved December 18, 2017. https://pubs.niaaa.nih.gov /publications/10report/chap04b.pdf.

National Institute on Alcohol Abuse and Alcoholism. "Underage Drinking." February 2017. https://pubs.niaaa.nih.gov /publications/UnderageDrinking/UnderageFact.htm.

Oswald, Anjelica. "Daniel Radcliffe Opens Up About His Struggle With Alcohol Addiction and Getting Sober." Business Insider, November 19, 2015. http://www.businessinsider.com /daniel-radcliffe-drinking-problem-2015-11.

Promises Treatment Center. "Which People Have the Highest Odds of Quitting Drinking?" July 18, 2014. https://www .promises.com/articles/alcoholism/highest-odds-to -quit-drinking.

Safe Communities Coalition. "10 Myths About Alcoholism." February 3, 2016. http://www.safecoalition .org/2016-02-03-10-myths-about-alcoholism.

Summit Behavioral Health. "Alcohol Addiction Experts Reveal What Happens to Your Body If You Stop Drinking." March 31, 2017. https://www.summitbehavioralhealth.com/blog /alcohol-addiction-experts-reveal-happens-body-stop -drinking.

Valby, Karen. "Demi Lovato Opens Up About Living Sober, Finding Her Voice & Feeling Confident." Refinery29, May 17, 2016. http://www.refinery29.com/2016/05/109501 /demi-lovato-confident-interview.

Winerip, Michael. Motherlode Blog. "Parents Offer Best Advice to Steer Clear of Teenage Drinking." *New York Times*, October 11, 2013. https://parenting.blogs.nytimes.com/2013/10/11 parents-offer-best-advice-to-steer-clear-of-teenage-drinking.

INDEX

ABOUT THE AUTHOR

Jennifer Peters is a writer and editor based in Washington, DC, where she is a researcher and data analyst with the News Media Alliance. She has written about relationships, food, books, and defense issues, with her work appearing in such outlets as *RT Book Reviews*, *Task & Purpose*, and *VICE News*. She is constantly in search of the perfect taco and a good book.

PHOTO CREDITS